4-24-13

To Kelsie Paige Haggard:

Congratulations on

your graduation!

Jim and June Brady

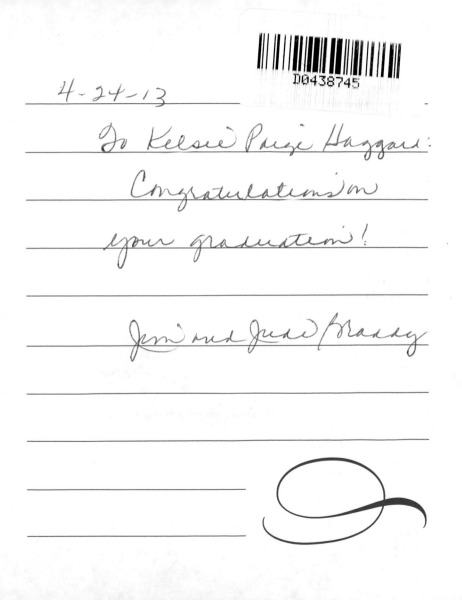

For Jonathan. . .

© 2004 by Barbour Publishing, Inc.

ISBN 1-59310-006-X

Cover image © PhotoDisc

Scripture quotations marked NKJV are taken from the New King James Version. Copyright © 1979, 1980, 1982 by Thomas Nelson, Inc. Used by permission. All rights reserved.

Scripture quotations marked KJV are taken from the King James Version of the Bible.

Scripture quotations marked NIV are taken from the HOLY BIBLE, NEW INTERNATIONAL VERSION®. NIV®. Copyright © 1973, 1978, 1984 by International Bible Society. Used by permission of Zondervan. All rights reserved.

Published by Humble Creek, P.O. Box 719, Uhrichsville, Ohio 44683

Printed in China.
5 4 3 2 1

101 TIPS FOR THE GRAD
WISDOM FOR THE LIFE AHEAD

Joanne Decker

HUMBLECREEK
INSPIRATION FOR LIFE

INTRODUCTION

Heartfelt congratulations as you reach one of life's great milestones—graduation day!

Ahead of you is the exciting continuation of this journey of life. Along life's road you will experience hopes, dreams, and joys as well as "bumps in the road" such as fear, anxiety, and possibly even failures. How you handle these experiences will determine the person you will ultimately become.

These *101 Tips for the Grad* are bits of wisdom from those who have traveled the bumpy road. . .dealt with it. . .learned from it. . .and moved on. May you benefit from these words of wisdom in ways that will make your life's journey more meaningful and worthwhile.

Enjoy the journey!

Blessings, love, and much joy always!

A wise man will hear and increase learning,
And a man of understanding will attain wise counsel.
PROVERBS 1:5 NKJV

MAKE THE MOST OF YOUR GOD-GIVEN TALENTS. 1.

Neglect not the gift that is in thee.
1 TIMOTHY 4:14 KJV

DARE TO DREAM. 2.

Where there is no vision, the people perish.
PROVERBS 29:18 KJV

LET FAITH BE YOUR GUIDE THROUGH LIFE'S TRIALS. 3.

Give thanks for sorrow that teaches you pity; for pain that teaches you
courage—and give exceeding thanks for the mystery which
remains a mystery still—the veil that hides you from the infinite, which
makes it possible for you to believe in what you cannot see.
ROBERT NATHAN

BE SURE YOUR HEART IS RIGHT, 4.
AND YOU'LL BE VERY WEALTHY.

Great beauty, great strength, and great riches are really and
truly of no great use; a right heart exceeds all.
BENJAMIN FRANKLIN

5. COUNT YOUR BLESSINGS.

Happiness will never come to those
who fail to appreciate what they already have.

AUTHOR UNKNOWN

6. DON'T TAKE EVERY CRITICISM TO HEART.

If I care to listen to every criticism, let alone act on them,
then this shop may as well be closed for all other businesses.
I have learned to do my best, and if the end result is good then
I do not care for any criticism, but if the end result is not good,
then even the praise of ten angels would not make the difference.

ABRAHAM LINCOLN

7. WORK WELL WITH OTHERS, EVEN WHEN THE SPOTLIGHT ISN'T ON YOU.

There is no limit to what can be accomplished
if it doesn't matter who gets the credit.

RALPH WALDO EMERSON

8. LOVE YOURSELF; LOVE OTHERS.

And now these three remain: faith, hope and love.
But the greatest of these is love.

1 CORINTHIANS 13:13 NIV

GIVE MORE THAN YOU GET, 9.
AND YOUR LIFE WILL BE FULL.

We make a living by what we get; we make a life by what we give.

SIR WINSTON CHURCHILL

STRIVE TO DO ALL THINGS WELL. 10.

Whatever you are, be a good one.

ABRAHAM LINCOLN

BE SINCERE; 11.
SAY ONLY WHAT YOU REALLY MEAN.

Well done is better than well said.

BENJAMIN FRANKLIN

IF YOU WANT TO BUILD GOOD CHARACTER, 12.
YOU MUST BE WILLING TO WORK.

You can't build a reputation on what you are going to do.

HENRY FORD

13. HAVE FAITH—IT GOES A LONG WAY.

The smallest seed of faith is better than the largest fruit of happiness.

HENRY DAVID THOREAU

14. THERE IS A TIME TO SPEAK UP AND A TIME TO KEEP QUIET. LEARN THE DIFFERENCE.

God is the friend of silence. Trees, flowers, grass grow in silence.
See the stars, moon, and sun how they move in silence.

MOTHER TERESA

15. ENDEAVOR TO OVERCOME THE OBSTACLES YOU ENCOUNTER IN LIFE.

A hero is an ordinary individual who finds the strength to persevere
and endure in spite of overwhelming obstacles.

CHRISTOPHER REEVE

16. SET YOUR SIGHTS ON ETERNAL REWARDS.

Each of us comes into life with fists closed, set for aggressiveness
and acquisition. But when we abandon life our hands are open;
there is nothing on earth that we need,
nothing the soul can take with it.

FULTON J. SHEEN

DETOUR

APPROACH ALL YOUR GOALS WITH 17. DETERMINATION AND PERSISTENCE.

Nothing in the world can take the place of persistence. Talent will not; nothing is more common than unsuccessful men with talent. Genius will not; unrewarded genius is almost a proverb. Education will not; the world is full of educated derelicts. Persistence and determination alone are omnipotent.
CALVIN COOLIDGE

DON'T BE SATISFIED WITH DOING 18. JUST ENOUGH TO GET BY.

Don't be content with doing only your duty. Do more than your duty. It's the horse that finishes a neck ahead wins the race.
ANDREW CARNEGIE

PRAY. . .AND BE PERSISTENT. 19.

Pray to God, but keep rowing to shore.
RUSSIAN PROVERB

ACCEPT RESPONSIBILITY. 20.

It is easier to do a job right than to explain why you didn't.
MARTIN VAN BUREN

21. STRIVE TO BE YOUR PERSONAL BEST.

Make the most of yourself, for that is all there is of you.

RALPH WALDO EMERSON

22. DARE TO BE DIFFERENT.

Let's dare to be ourselves, for we do that better than anyone else.

SHIRLEY BRIGGS

23. WHEN GOD SHOWS YOU HIS WILL, ACT UPON IT.

Do not ask the Lord to guide your footsteps
if you are not willing to move your feet.

AUTHOR UNKNOWN

24. REALIZE THAT GOD HAS A PURPOSE FOR EVERYTHING.

Sorrow is a fruit. God does not allow it to grow
on a branch that is too weak to bear it.

VICTOR HUGO

25. FIND SOLUTIONS—NOT EXCUSES.

Ninety-nine percent of the failures come from people
who have the habit of making excuses.

GEORGE WASHINGTON CARVER

ONE WAY

HELP OTHERS. 26.

The life of the individual only has meaning insofar as it aids in making
the life of every living thing nobler and more beautiful. Life is sacred, that
is to say, it is the supreme value to which all other values are subordinate.
ALBERT EINSTEIN

MAKE YOUR OWN WAY. 27.

If there is no wind, row.
LATIN PROVERB

ENCOURAGE OTHERS IN THEIR ENDEAVORS. 28.

Great people are those who can make others feel
that they, too, can become great.
MARK TWAIN

LEAD BY EXAMPLE. 29.

Example is not the main thing in influencing others.
It is the only thing.
ALBERT SCHWEITZER

30. WHEN YOUR IDEA SEEMS IMPOSSIBLE, TURN AWAY FROM DISCOURAGEMENT.

Nearly every man who develops an idea works at it up to
the point where it looks impossible, and then gets discouraged.
That's not the place to become discouraged.

THOMAS EDISON

31. TRUE FRIENDS STAND BY YOU IN GOOD TIMES AND IN BAD—BE A GOOD FRIEND.

Friendships multiply joys and divide griefs.

H. G. BOHN

32. FORGIVE OTHERS IF YOU WANT TO BE FORGIVEN.

He who cannot forgive others destroys
the bridge over which he himself must pass.

GEORGE HERBERT

33. HAVE COURAGE TO STAND UP TO LIFE'S OBSTACLES; THEY'RE NOT AS STRONG AS YOU THINK.

Stand up to your obstacles and do something about them.
You will find that they haven't half the strength you think they have.

NORMAN VINCENT PEALE

WORK AT OVERCOMING YOUR DOUBTS. 34.

Our doubts are traitors and make us lose
the good we oft might win by fearing to attempt.
WILLIAM SHAKESPEARE

COMBINE WISDOM, KNOWLEDGE, 35.
AND SKILL IN YOUR WORK.

If you are wise, your wisdom will reward you.
PROVERBS 9:12 NIV

HAVE THE COURAGE TO SAY "NO." 36.

Saying no to something is actually
much more powerful than saying yes.
TOM HANKS

USE WHAT YOU HAVE FOR THE GOOD OF OTHERS. 37.

Fame is a four-letter word. And like tape, or zoom, or face, or pain,
or love, or life, what ultimately matters is what we do with it.
FRED ROGERS

38. TRUST IN THE LORD, AND HE WILL DELIVER YOU.

Do not be anxious abut anything, but in everything, by prayer
and petition, with thanksgiving, present your requests to God.

PHILIPPIANS 4:6 NIV

39. DON'T LOOK FOR HAPPINESS IN THE WRONG PLACES.

Delight yourself in the LORD and
he will give you the desires of your heart.

PSALM 37:4 NIV

40. LOOK TO YOUR CREATOR FOR GUIDANCE.

Teach me to do your will, for you are my God.

PSALM 143:10 NIV

41. DON'T LET YOUR INNER CHILD GROW OLD.

We need the enthusiasm of the young. We need their
joie de vivre. In it is reflected something of the
original joy God had in creating man.

POPE JOHN PAUL II

KNOW THAT GOD HAS 42.
YOUR BEST INTEREST AT HEART.

Know when God gives you what you NEED instead of what you want.
JOANNE DECKER

BE HAPPY WITH WHO YOU ARE. 43.

Learn to enjoy your own company. You are the one person
you can count on living with for the rest of your life.
AUTHOR UNKNOWN

NEVER LOSE SIGHT OF WHAT IS IMPORTANT. 44.

The ability to focus attention on important things is
a defining characteristic of intelligence.
ROBERT J. SHILLER

DETERMINE TO REACH THE 45.
SEEMINGLY UNATTAINABLE GOALS.

So many of our dreams seem impossible, then improbable, then inevitable.
CHRISTOPHER REEVE

NEVER GIVE UP. 46.

Persistence trumps talent and looks every time.
AARON BROWN

47. DON'T LIVE IN THE PAST.

Keep moving if you love life, and keep your troubles well behind you.

JOHN MCCAIN

48. ENDURE THE PAIN THAT SOMETIMES PRECEDES SUCCESS.

Reach for the stars, even if you have to stand on a cactus.

SUSAN LONGACRE

49. DON'T PLACE LIMITS ON YOURSELF.

The best way to get people to think out of the box
is not to create the box in the first place.

MARTIN COOPER

50. BE THANKFUL FOR WHAT YOU HAVE.

Give thanks to the LORD, for he is good.

PSALM 136:1 NIV

51. EVERYTHING YOU DO, DO WITH EVERYTHING YOU HAVE.

Joy comes from using your potential.

WILL SCHULTZ

DETOUR

ONE WAY

HAVE FAITH IN EVEN THE UNSEEN THINGS OF GOD. 52.

When you come to the edge of all the light you know and are about to step off into the darkness of the unknown, faith is knowing one of two things will happen: There will be something solid to stand on or you will be taught how to fly.

BARBARA J. WINTER

STOP AND SMELL THE ROSES. 53.

Reflect upon your present blessings, of which every man has many— not on your past misfortunes, of which all men have some.

CHARLES DICKENS

WORK HARD AND EXPERIENCE SATISFYING VICTORY. 54.

Men talk as if victory were something fortunate. Work is victory.

RALPH WALDO EMERSON

ALWAYS LOOK FOR OPPORTUNITY IN 55. THE DIFFICULT THINGS OF LIFE.

A pessimist sees the difficulty in every opportunity; an optimist sees the opportunity in every difficulty.

SIR WINSTON CHURCHILL

56. LOOK FOR OPPORTUNITY IN THE MOST UNEXPECTED PLACES.

Many an opportunity is lost because a man is out looking for four-leaf clovers.

ANONYMOUS

57. DON'T LET YOUR FEARS STAND IN THE WAY OF YOUR DREAMS.

One of the greatest discoveries a man makes, one of his great surprises, is to find he can do what he was afraid he couldn't do.

HENRY FORD

58. REMEMBER, LITTLE THINGS MEAN A LOT, TOO.

Character may be manifested in the great moments, but it is made in the small ones.

PHILLIP BROOKS

59. DARE TO DO THE RIGHT THING.

Always do right; this will gratify some people and astonish the rest.

MARK TWAIN

DETOUR

ACCEPT CONSTRUCTIVE CRITICISM. 60.

A successful person is one who can lay a firm foundation
with the bricks that others throw at him or her.
DAVID BRINKLEY

LIGHT A FIRE IN YOUR HEART. 61.

Nothing great was ever achieved without enthusiasm.
RALPH WALDO EMERSON

REALIZE THAT THE PATH LESS 62.
TRAVELED IS OFTEN THE BETTER CHOICE.

Do not go where the path may lead,
go instead where there is no path and leave a trail.
RALPH WALDO EMERSON

HAVE FAITH IN THE LORD, 63.
AND YOU WILL ALWAYS SEE THE LIGHT.

Keep your face to the sunshine and you cannot see the shadow.
HELEN KELLER

64. WHEN NECESSARY, BE STRONG ENOUGH TO GO AGAINST THE FLOW.

Any intelligent fool can make things bigger, more complex, and more violent. It takes a touch of genius—and a lot of courage—to move in the opposite direction.

ALBERT EINSTEIN

65. ALWAYS STRIVE FOR EXCELLENCE.

The secret of joy in work is contained in one word—EXCELLENCE. To know how to do something well is to enjoy it.

PEARL BUCK

66. BE OPTIMISTIC.

An optimist is someone who goes after Moby Dick in a rowboat and takes the tartar sauce with him.

ZIG ZIGLAR

67. BE CONFIDENT WITH WHO YOU ARE.

Class is an aura of confidence that is being sure without being cocky. Class has nothing to do with money. Class never runs scared. It is self-discipline and self-knowledge. It's the sure-footedness that comes with having proved you can meet life.

ANN LANDERS

DON'T MEASURE YOUR SUCCESS BY 68. YOUR MATERIAL WEALTH.

Always demanding the best of oneself, living with honor,
devoting one's talents and gifts to the benefits of others—
these are the measures of success that endure
when material things have passed away.
GERALD R. FORD

BE THOUGHTFUL AND CONSIDERATE OF OTHERS. 69.

All the gold in the world has no significance. That which is
lasting are the thoughtful acts which we do for our fellow man.
ADOLFO PRIETO

LOOK FORWARD TO TOMORROW. 70.

Finish each day and be done with it. You have done what you could.
Some blunders and absurdities no doubt crept in; forget them as
soon as you can. Tomorrow is a new day; begin it well and serenely
and with too high a spirit to be cumbered with your old nonsense.
RALPH WALDO EMERSON

71. GO AHEAD. . .TAKE A STEP OUT OF YOUR COMFORT ZONE.

Be brave enough to live life creatively. The creative is the place where no one else has ever been. You have to leave the city of your comfort and go into the wilderness of your intuition. You can't get there by bus, only by hard work and risk and by not quite knowing what you're doing. What you'll discover will be wonderful. What you'll discover will be yourself.

ALAN ALDA

72. DREAM BIG.

We grow great by dreams. All big men are dreamers. They see things in the soft haze of a spring day or in the red fire of a long winter's evening. Some of us let these great dreams die, but others nourish and protect them; nurse them through bad days till they bring them to the sunshine and light which comes always to those who sincerely hope that their dreams will come true.

WOODROW WILSON

73. TAKE ACTION OR RISK MISSING OPPORTUNITIES FOR PROGRESS.

There are risks and costs to action. But they are far less than the long-range risks of comfortable inaction.

JOHN F. KENNEDY

NEVER LOSE SIGHT OF WHO YOU TRULY ARE. 74.

To be nobody but yourself—in a world which is doing its best, night and day, to make you like everybody else—means to fight the hardest battle which any human being can fight, and never stop fighting.
E. E. CUMMINGS

KNOW WHEN YOU'VE "OUTGROWN" YOURSELF. 75.

You may not realize it when it happens, but a kick in the teeth may be the best thing in the world for you.
WALT DISNEY

DON'T LET PEER PRESSURE SWAY YOUR JUDGMENT. 76.

Right is right, even if everyone is against it;
and wrong is wrong, even if everyone is for it.
WILLIAM PENN

IF YOU WISH TO SUCCEED, 77.
YOU MUST WORK TOWARD SUCCESS.

The only place where success comes before work is in a dictionary.
VIDAL SASSOON

25

78. CHOOSE PEOPLE OF GOOD CHARACTER TO BE YOUR FRIENDS.

Associate yourself with men of good quality if you esteem your own reputation; for it is better to be alone than in bad company.

GEORGE WASHINGTON

79. RISE ABOVE LIFE'S DIFFICULTIES.

Little minds are tamed and subdued by misfortune; but great minds rise above them.

WASHINGTON IRVING

80. WORK MORE THAN YOU WORRY.

The reason why worry kills more people than work is that more people worry than work.

ROBERT FROST

81. LET A POSITIVE ATTITUDE BE YOUR DRIVING FORCE.

Nothing on earth can stop the man with the right mental attitude from achieving his goals; nothing on earth can help the man with the wrong mental attitude.

THOMAS JEFFERSON

ALLOW TIMES OF ADVERSITY TO **82.** POSITIVELY AFFECT YOUR CHARACTER.

Great people aren't those who are happy at times of convenience and content, but of how they are in times of catastrophe and controversy.
MARTIN LUTHER KING JR.

DON'T BE CONTENT WITH THE STATUS QUO. **83.**

Even if you are on the right track, you'll get run over if you just sit there.
WILL ROGERS

MAKE DOING YOUR BEST A PERSONAL HABIT. **84.**

We are what we repeatedly do. Excellence, then, is not an act but a habit.
ARISTOTLE

USE YOUR FAILURES TO FUEL **85.** YOUR DRIVE TO SUCCEED.

I have missed more than 9,000 shots in my career. I have lost almost 300 games. On 26 occasions I have been entrusted to take the game winning shot. . .and I missed. I have failed over and over and over again in my life. And that's precisely why I succeed.
MICHAEL JORDAN

86. KEEP YOUR ATTITUDE IN CHECK.

Your attitude about who you are and what you have
is a very little thing that makes a very big difference.

THEODORE ROOSEVELT

87. NEVER LOSE SIGHT OF YOUR GOALS.

The spirit, the will to win, and the will to excel are the things that endure.
These qualities are so much more important than the events that occur.

VINCE LOMBARDI

88. KNOW WHEN TO LISTEN TO YOUR HEART.

The snob's error is to put good taste before a good heart.

JOSEPH EPSTEIN

89. DON'T WORRY ABOUT THE THINGS YOU CAN'T CONTROL.

Cast your cares on the LORD and he will sustain you;
he will never let the righteous fall.

PSALM 55:22 NIV

HAVE AN "I CAN" ATTITUDE. 90.

Whether you think that you can, or that you can't, you are usually right.

HENRY FORD

DON'T PUT OFF 'TIL TOMORROW 91.
WHAT YOU CAN ACCOMPLISH TODAY.

Someday is not a day of the week.

AUTHOR UNKNOWN

HOLD ON TO HOPE. 92.

There is surely a future hope for you.

PROVERBS 23:18 NIV

DON'T LET INHIBITIONS HOLD YOU BACK. 93.

Twenty years from now you will be more disappointed by the
things that you didn't do than by the ones you did do. So throw
off the bowlines. Sail away from the safe harbor. Catch the
trade winds in your sails. Explore. Dream. Discover.

MARK TWAIN

29

94. LEARN TO BE TOLERANT.

We could learn a lot from crayons: Some are sharp, some are pretty; some are dull, while others bright; some have weird names, but we have to learn how to live in the same box.

AUTHOR UNKNOWN

95. FIND VALUE IN EACH PART OF LIFE'S JOURNEY.

Often the search proves more profitable than the goal.

E. L. KONIGSBURG

96. ALWAYS HOLD ON TO YOUR DREAMS.

Hold fast to dreams for if dreams die, life is a broken winged bird that cannot fly.

LANGSTON HUGHES

97. BE CONFIDENT.

You can achieve anything you want in life if you have the courage to dream it, the intelligence to make a realistic plan, and the will to see that plan through to the end.

SIDNEY A. FRIEDMAN